Jeff Buehner

The Sultan's Seven Secrets

One

Silent
Navigator

I'm going to tell you a story that you should have heard a long time ago, and I'm going to tell you exactly why you haven't heard it until now.

I heard this story at a time when I badly needed the circumstances of my life to change but had no idea what to do to make that change happen. I felt helpless, powerless and out of control.

Because of this story, almost every aspect of my life changed in a dramatic and positive way. And, the change happened so rapidly that it shocked members of my family, many of my friends and above all, ME! I went from feeling helpless and miserable, to knowing exactly how to seize control of my future... and that's what I did!

At the time I heard this story, I was thirty three years old, and worked as a concrete contractor. My every waking hour was spent trying to provide a decent life for my growing family... and somehow always falling just a little short. The financial pressure I felt was suffocating me!

As a concrete contractor, my alarm went off every morning at five thirty and I'd wake up thinking, "Crap, I'm still alive!"

My days were spent pouring and finishing concrete, setting forms for the next pour, selling new jobs and collecting money. I'd get home every night just in time to wolf down my dinner, shower and fall into bed so I could do it all over again the next day. It got to the point where I viewed life as a punishment instead of a blessing. I bet you've felt that way before too.

Looking back, I realize that I had a tremendous amount to be thankful for but exhaustion, physical pain, constant worry and the crushing financial pressure made it difficult for me to feel anything but mild panic.

One day, while setting forms with my crew, an elderly woman came out of the house we were working on and handed me a manuscript. She told me to read it that night and give it back to her the next morning.

She said I could talk about the story all I wanted from memory and notes but asked me not to make a copy of the manuscript. As she handed me the document, I thought, "Lady, there is no way on earth that I have time to read your paper." But I just smiled, thanked her and hurriedly put the manuscript in my truck so I could get back to work.

I had no way of knowing, in that moment, that my prayers for a better life had just been answered!

That evening as I cleaned out my truck I took the manuscript into the house and put it on the night stand. A few hours later, while waiting for my wife to come to bed I picked it up and read the first page... and didn't put it down until I was finished.

The manuscript told the story of the author of the famous fairy tale that we're all acquainted with, Aladdin and the Magic Lamp. The author is a real man in documented history named Sultan Musa of Mali who lived in West Africa around 1300 A.D. Sultan Musa of Mali was the richest man to ever walk the earth. His wealth is estimated at eight hundred billion dollars... eight times the wealth of Jeff Bezos of Amazon fame. Sultan Musa of Mali's wealth estimates fluctuate because they're based on the current value of gold... because that's what Musa had, tons and tons of gold.

Musa was not born the son of a Sultan. In fact, his father died when Musa was a very young boy. Being fatherless in West Africa around 1300 A.D. meant tremendous hardship and Musa knew little else. His days were filled with bouts of intermittent excitement and terror. To survive, he and his little band of street urchin friends stole what they needed from local farmers and merchants. Musa lived with the ever present knowledge that he could be caught at any moment and severely beaten, which happened many times.

At the age of twelve, Musa fell in with an older thief. This thief had secretly followed a wealthy merchant into the countryside and had spied on him as he moved a stone on the ground and descended by rope ladder into a cavern. When the merchant emerged, he carried with him what the thief accurately assumed were bags of gold.

The older thief recruited Musa to be his partner because Musa was small enough to be lowered into the cave by rope and to be pulled up again. Once in the cave, Musa loaded bag after bag of riches until the last bag had been hauled to the surface. Musa then called to his partner to pull him up.

Of course, the older thief did not hand down the rope again but moved the stone back into place leaving Musa to die… which he did.

After several days without food or water Musa perished and had what we call today, a near death experience. During this out-of-body experience he met a man "made of light" who taught him many astonishing things. One of the things he taught Musa is that he had two bodies, a physical body and a spirit body. His spirit body was made of very real material that is infinitely superior to the material that made up his physical body. He learned that his spirit body is immortal and can never die. Musa learned that his spirit body is literally a child of God.

The man made of light also taught Musa that he had two minds working simultaneously, a conscious mind and a subconscious mind. The subconscious mind is connected to all power, all knowledge and all wisdom but it limits the amount of knowledge and wisdom it shares with the conscious mind to just what the conscious mind needs to play a specific role. To understand this relationship better, it's helpful to view the conscious mind as an actor on a stage and the subconscious mind as a highly efficient stage manager. The actor gets into a specific role and is dedicated to staying in character. The subconscious mind helps the actor stay in character by setting the stage with everything necessary to support that role… and nothing that might detract from playing that particular role. It is designed this way so an individual can gain experience and understanding from playing various roles.

Musa realized that street urchin and petty thief were just roles he'd been playing on earth. Those roles were by no means the limit of who Musa was.

By the way, you and I are doing the same thing. We're just playing roles that our conscious minds are dedicated to. We think of our roles as who we are but it's not really true. We can drop our current role and choose a different role at any time.

To illustrate this point, consider the fact that if you had been born a hundred and fifty years ago into an Apache tribe you would be just as dedicated to being an Apache as you are dedicated today to being you. You may currently be worried about building your bank account and 401k or fighting racism or changing the world or whatever it is you're about but as an Apache, none of those things would be the least bit important to you. You would be thoroughly consumed with hunting, skinning, gathering and probably killing enemies. You'd be hard pressed to think of yourself as anything but an Apache Indian but the fact is, you'd just be playing the role of Apache, nothing more, nothing less. You have the capacity to play many widely varying roles, millions of roles! Your surroundings obviously influence the roles you choose to play but you can change your role within the confines of your surroundings any time you want. You can also, in many cases, change your surroundings. We'll talk more about this shortly, but back to Musa's story.

Musa was taught that his subconscious mind supported the role he played by feeding him feelings and impulses and by manipulating situations and circumstances to keep him fully engaged in that role. Musa learned that he was free to choose any role he was capable of dreaming up.

He also learned that to change his role all he had to do was communicate his will to his powerful subconscious mind and his subconscious mind would instantly and happily honor his will. Let me repeat that. **THE SUBCONSCIOUS MIND HONORS YOUR WILL!** It is a willing servant. It has always honored your will... and make no mistake, you've chosen your current role. You've been telling your subconscious mind what your role is since childhood... and like a silent navigator, it has expertly guided your life along the course *you* plotted. Now, it's fair to assume that you haven't been fully aware of how this communication has been taking place, but you're about to learn, and this knowledge can change your life forever.

It's no wonder that when Musa wrote the metaphor of his life, Aladdin and the Magic Lamp, that he would compare his subconscious mind to an all-powerful Genie. To Musa, the incredible power and ability wielded by the subconscious mind must have seemed nothing less than magical.

Musa learned that he could seize control of his life by *consciously* speaking to his silent navigator in the language it hears and responds to. The man made of light taught Musa this language and Musa referred to it as the "Language of the Gods." Having learned this language, Musa was in the position to tell his subconscious mind exactly what kind of life to create for him. In that moment, he became Sultan of his own destiny!

Eventually the man made of light told Musa that he had go back, that he had a work to do among his people and he assured Musa that he would find his way out of the cave.

The next thing Musa knew, he awoke in the dark cave and instantly broke into a cold sweat. It was pitch black all around him. He couldn't see anything. The cool breeze on his clammy face made it feel cold and wet. Then he realized that if there was a breeze, air was moving through the cave, which meant there must be other openings. Musa inched forward on his hands and knees, keeping his face to the breeze until he came to a small hole which he was able to enlarge and eventually squeeze through.

Musa staggered from the cave in a state of near deadly dehydration. Just before passing out, he heard the gurgle of a small stream. He fell to his knees and drank the cool, clear water. In that moment, no human being's physical reality could have been on a lower plane. He was barely alive. He owned nothing. He was a criminal. He had no father, no safety net, no opportunity and no prospects... yet Musa was filled to overflowing with joy and excitement! He'd been given a second chance at life and although he was the poorest of men, he carried in his heart a priceless secret.

By employing what he'd been taught by the man made of light, Musa dreamed up a different role to play. He chose to play the role of an extremely wealthy, honorable, kind and wise merchant. He then communicated his will to his subconscious mind in the Language of the Gods, whereupon his subconscious mind instantly obeyed him and began manipulating the circumstances of Musa's life accordingly.

In the next chapter, I will teach you to speak this language... the Language of the Gods. If you're anything like me, you'll notice some extremely surprising changes take place, even as you just dabble and experiment with speaking it.

To become a wealthy merchant, Musa had to first get involved in trade. So, he lent himself out as a camel driver to a merchant who traded in salt and gold. Due to his honesty, good nature and desire to learn, Musa soon became the merchant's most valued driver and also became trusted and loved by all who came to know him. Eventually, the merchant taught Musa the art of finding mineral deposits. Musa was a quick-study, and over time he came to own some of the largest and most productive gold and salt mines in all of West Africa. With the first gold Musa acquired, he paid back the man he and the older thief had stolen from tenfold, meaning he gave the man ten times the amount of gold that he had helped steal from him.

Musa was so dedicated to following the teachings of the man made of light that everywhere he went he gave generously to the poor and downtrodden. In 1324, the Egyptian historian Shihab al Umari recorded that when Musa traveled through Cairo on his way to Mecca, he gave away so much gold to the peasants who ran out to meet his impressive caravan that it temporarily collapsed the Egyptian economy. One can actually read of this account in history books.

But Musa didn't just give gold. He built schools and instructed teachers to teach students, young and old, how to use their God-given gifts and abilities to create happy, healthy and prosperous lives. By so doing, he substantially increased the wealth, general happiness and overall standard of living in the entire Mali kingdom.

It was common in those days for Sultans to choose a deputy to rule in their absence if they left the kingdom for any reason. The current Sultan determined to lead an exploration to find the boundaries of the Atlantic Ocean and chose Musa to be his deputy until he returned. He chose Musa because Musa was well known for his honesty, wisdom, and of course his independent wealth. In addition, the people already knew and loved Musa because of his goodness and generosity and they were happy to obey him.

The Sultan never returned from his adventures and Musa remained Sultan to the end of his days.

Sultan Musa of Mali wrote the story of his life in two parts. The first part is a metaphor for his life, the tale of Aladdin and the Magic Lamp. But the second part is a detailed interpretation of the fairy tale. It details who the Genie is and what the Magic Lamp represents. It gives a precise tutorial in speaking the Language of the Gods, which allowed Musa to transform his life from that of a poor, wretched street urchin to the life of an unbelievably wealthy merchant and finally Sultan over the entire Mali Kingdom.

Musa was clear about his intent. He wrote about his life and about his transformation so that you, the reader, could learn to take control of your reality and transform your life, just like he did.

Musa shared the fairy tale with anyone who would listen but the second part, the interpretation, Musa was careful to share only with those he trusted because even sultans can get into trouble if they start sounding crazy.

Now, fast forward three hundred years. In the 1600s, a man named Antoine Galland translated and published the stories of Sinbad the Sailor and 1001 Arabian nights from original Arabic texts. He didn't write these stories, he just translated and published them. One day he was given two more texts by a Syrian fisherman, the tale of Aladdin and the Magic Lamp and the complete interpretation of the fairytale, both written by Sultan Musa of Mali.

Galland translated these texts but only published the fairy tale. He didn't publish the interpretation because it talked of God, spirit bodies, out of body experiences and an array of spiritual things. Galland was terrified that if he published the interpretation he might be labeled "mad" by his peers in academia and government, which would ruin his career and possibly cost him his life. Remember, in Europe, around this time, people were burned at the stake for the crime of heresy!

Galland kept the interpretation safely locked away. The interpretation was passed down from generation to generation but as far as I know, the original text has never been formally published.

This is why I often refer to this story as **"the greatest story never told."**

When I read the manuscript of the interpretation and was presented with the idea that Aladdin and the Magic Lamp was, in concept, true... that each of us has an all-powerful Genie inside of us who can create a life filled with success, wealth and happiness, I was thrilled beyond words!

The story of Sultan Musa of Mali rattled around in my head for a few days. I didn't do much differently except think about what I'd read. My current role as concrete contractor still consumed my every waking hour. Then one day it began to rain. It rained for days on end and I couldn't work. The longer it rained the more worried about my financial situation I became. As I angrily looked out the window at the falling rain one morning, the phone rang. A friend had called to invite me to lunch.

At lunch, I unloaded my problems and frustrations onto him. I told him about how hard I worked, how exhausted I was, how difficult it was to stay afloat in business and how down and depressed I felt. He's a really good friend so he just listened for about twenty minutes without interrupting me and then he finally said, "Show me how you do down and depressed."

I was confused by his question and said, "I don't do down and depressed, I am down and depressed."

He said, "No, I'm talking about your physicality... for example you've rounded your shoulders and draped your upper body over the table as if you lack the strength to hold yourself up. You've also let your face sag and made your eyes droopy."

I looked at him incredulously and felt myself getting mad! But before I could say anything, he said. "I want you to play a little game if you don't mind." Before I could respond, he continued.

"Pretend for a moment that your long lost Aunt calls and explains that she doesn't have long to live, that she would like to see you again before she goes and what's more, she wants to give you two million dollars. All you have to do to get your check for two million dollars is to be at her home in Florida by tomorrow night at seven o'clock."

"Now," He said. "Tell me everything you'd have to do to get to Florida by tomorrow night."

Because he is such a good friend and because I knew his intentions were good, I decided to play along.

"I'd have to get an airplane ticket, which will be expensive on short notice... but who cares, I'm getting two million dollars, right? We'd need to get a baby sitter... unless I decided not to tell my wife about the money and went to Florida alone. If I did that, I could stop by the Lexus dealership on the way home and surprise her with the SUV she's always wanted. Can you even imagine the look on her face if I pulled up in a brand new Lexus SUV and handed her the keys?!", I asked.

"Freeze!" He said. "Look at yourself! In less than thirty seconds you went from wearing a sad, droopy face and needing the table to support your body weight, to sitting up straight and tall with bright, flashing eyes, a smile on your face, talking excitedly and breathing deeply."

"You see?" He continued. "You can **do** down and depressed, or you can **do** pumped up and excited, all based on the thoughts and scenarios you choose to entertain in your mind. But know this;

Whichever you choose to do, life will bring you more of it."

I just sat there blinking for what must have seemed like an unnaturally long time.

Finally, I blurted out, "You're absolutely right! That's exactly how it works, isn't it?!" My friend smiled and nodded his head.

In that moment the teachings in Sultan Musa of Mali's manuscript came into crystal clear focus for me. I knew exactly how to turn my life around. Thrilled beyond anything I had experienced in years, I rushed home and took the imagination game I'd just played with my friend to a whole new level!

With pen and paper in hand, I dreamed up all kinds of amazing possibilities and literally redesigned my entire life. I dreamed up a brand new role and spelled it out in as much detail as possible. Then I tore up magazines and cut out pictures that depicted and supported my new role... my new life! I pasted these pictures onto sheets of paper and wrote statements that defined the new role I was determined to play. Some of the things I dreamed up were utterly fantastic and far-fetched. Some things were quite plausible but whether fantastic or plausible, they all had one thing in common... they got me sizzling with excitement!

I then began speaking to my subconscious mind in the Language of the Gods as taught to me by Sultan Musa of Mali. As I did, I noticed the occurrence of several odd coincidences. As I went from being tired, surly and cross to literally bounding out of bed every morning with a smile on my face, feeling energetic and happy and anticipating each new day like a child anticipates Christmas, I noticed that people responded differently to me. Selling new jobs became noticeably easier. People started begging me to do their work. Instead of hounding people for the money they owed me, it seemed like they now happily handed it over.

I was still a concrete contractor. I still had to get up at five thirty in the morning, leave the house by six thirty and pour concrete all day. But while my physical body was setting forms and finishing cement, my mind was filled with dreams of fabulous possibilities. I'd dream I was building my own home on a tropical island or that I was an extremely successful, young entrepreneur, passionately delivering a presentation to a crowd of very important people. I didn't know exactly what I was pitching, but at the end of my presentation I imagined all of those important people jumping to their feet clapping and cheering! As they clapped and cheered, it meant that I was going to make a LOT of money! I envisioned millions of dollars pouring into my bank account and spent a substantial part of each day figuring out what I was going to do with all my money!

I found that some people were shocked by even these early changes that had come over me. One day while finishing a pad of concrete and whistling a happy tune, I noticed my foreman staring at me. Finally, I stopped whistling and asked, "What?" Then he asked, "What are you so &@%# happy about?" He didn't mean it in a derogatory way. He was just curious. Concrete guys don't typically act the way I was acting. He wanted to know if I was having an affair. I assured him that I wasn't having an affair and tried my best to explain what I was doing. He answered by saying, "Whatever floats your boat, Dude."

The shock he and others around me were experiencing now was

about to become a lot more pronounced!

I didn't know for sure that any of the things I was imagining would come true in my physical world, but focusing on exciting imaginary scenarios got me pumped up... and I liked it!

I never went anywhere without a "Dream Sheet" in my back pocket. As I drove my old pickup truck from job site to job site, I'd lay the Dream Sheet on the dash board or the seat next to me and glance at the pictures from time to time and pretend that this was my life. My fantastic dreams made me feel exceptionally happy and hopeful, and I liked feeling that way! It certainly felt better than dwelling on my difficult and sometimes depressing reality. Soon, I noticed weird coincidences occurring that led to a shift in my reality... a shift toward the dreams I was focusing on in my imagination. Let me tell you about one of these coincidences.

While eating lunch with my crew one day, I noticed the wife of an old friend from college sitting with her friends. Normally I would have slipped out the back hoping not to be seen in my dirty work clothes but things had changed. In my mind, I was a successful, young, gregarious and outgoing entrepreneur. I walked right up to her and asked how my old friend, her husband, was doing and expressed a desire to see him again. She gave me his number and the next time it rained I invited him to lunch. At lunch we talked about business ideas.

My friend told me that he'd worked as a relatively low-level employee at a large, national marketing firm that sold home-based business opportunities to people all over the country. He mused that if I knew of a way for people to make five hundred dollars or more in passive income, we could pitch our idea to the marketing company and have a very successful new business.

I said, "I can do a lot better than $500 per month!" Then I told him that before my wife and I moved back to Utah to start our family, we lived in Southern California. On rainy days, when I couldn't pour concrete, I'd place gumball-style vending machines filled with delicious Swedish Mints in up-scale restaurants. My route grew to twelve machines before we moved back to Utah, but that little route of twelve machines generated $2,400 in net revenue every month!

My friend was astonished! He asked more questions about the vending business, and the more I answered his questions, the more excited he became.

He asked me to put together a presentation for the marketing company and he set up an appointment for me to deliver it. Soon, I found myself in a room filled with the top-level executives of the national marketing company waiting my turn to pitch our home-based business idea centered on the vending business. I'd brought one of the vending machines I was going to talk about with me. The machine was painted gold and it sat atop a beautifully stained and lacquered wood stand. It was filled with colorful Swedish Mints. My wife had sown a cloak out of black fabric which concealed the machine until I was ready to reveal it.

There were three people who had been invited to pitch ideas and I was scheduled to go last. The first guy got up and began pitching his idea. Almost immediately a member of the marketing team asked a very pointed question that seemed to stump the presenter. This touched off a barrage of harsh criticism and more difficult questions. The presenter became flustered. He didn't have good answers, and within just a few minutes, he was abruptly dismissed. As he sheepishly gathered his things and made an awkward exit, the second guy got up and began talking. The same thing happened to him! He was eaten alive, figuratively speaking, and summarily sent away.

By this point, I had begun to question the validity of our idea and had lost a considerable amount of confidence in it. In my heart, I was wishing I could get out of making the presentation. Just then, the President of the company said, "Let's take a fifteen minute bathroom break and then we'll hear what Mr. Buehner has to say."

Everyone got up and left the room. I was about to make a dash for my truck when I decided instead to reach back and touch my pocket. In that pocket, I had a folded up dream sheet. As I remembered the statements and pictures on that sheet, I instantly snapped into the state of young, successful entrepreneur that my dream sheet provoked! The vending business had been good to me. The extra income gave my wife and me a great deal of security and I decided to pitch my idea with confidence and passion. If they didn't like it, so be it.

When the meeting reconvened, I placed my cloaked vending machine on the corner of the large conference room table and began talking about the importance of owning high rate-of-return income producing assets. I talked about how each of the assets I was talking about cost roughly $150 to buy but made me, on average, $200 every month... more than enough to buy another one just like it! That's a nearly 1600% annual rate of return! I referred to these assets as my fleet of "Silent Salesmen," and told them that by owning just twelve of these Silent Salesmen, I made $2,400 net revenue every month! Servicing my fleet required just two or three hours every Saturday morning. At the end of the presentation, I asked if they wanted to see one of these "Silent Salesmen," and in unison they all shouted, "Yes!" So, I jerked the cloak off of my vending machine and everyone in the room jumped to their feet clapping and cheering!

The President of the company came up to me and said, "Bring your partner to my office tomorrow at ten o'clock. We've got a lot to talk about."

Just like that, I had a new business, a new, fun partner and a new, much more exciting and rewarding life... and (not insignificantly) began making a LOT of money! With the new money I was making, it wasn't long before I owned (in real-life) the new car I'd been driving in my imagination for the past several months. Shortly after that, the new home I'd been living in (in my imagination), became a reality. And, a lot of other exciting things changed too.

The speedy transformation of my life shocked a lot of my friends and family members. And, the speed at which it happened surprised me too! But, **how it happened** didn't surprise me at all. I knew exactly what I'd done to cause the change.

I had dreamed up the new role I wanted to play, consciously communicated my desires to my subconscious mind in the Language of the Gods... and the silent navigator of my destiny took it from there. It was as simple as that.

So what is this "Language of the Gods" and, can *you* learn to speak it? The answer is, "Yes you can!" And, I want to teach it to you right now!

Notes

Notes

Two

Language of the Gods

In Sultan Musa of Mali's metaphor, Aladdin and the Magic Lamp, Aladdin represents the *conscious* mind.

The all-powerful Genie represents the **subconscious** mind.

The Magic Lamp represents the language the Genie hears and responds to. You see, your subconscious mind does not listen to the words that come out of your mouth or even the thoughts in your head. You don't always say what you mean and your thoughts can be so scattered at times that you can't even keep them straight. Your subconscious mind operates on a much simpler, more primitive and much more reliable mechanism: **FEELINGS!** This is the language of the Gods!

Your subconscious mind hears, responds to and is programmed by the predominant feelings you experience moment by moment and day by day. Once you take control of how and what you feel, you take control of the communication between your conscious and subconscious minds. Once you control this communication, you can do what Musa did and what I did, namely seize control of your reality and your future.

Your subconscious mind controls every aspect of your life and does it with incredible power and precision. It decides if you're bold and confident or nervous and shy. It determines whether you're highly motivated and successful or flat out lazy and unproductive. It decides if you're full of energy or tired all the time. Your subconscious mind even dictates how lovable and attractive you are, which ideas pop into your head, how much money you'll make and whether you'll have a fun, exciting and fulfilling life or live out your days in quiet misery.

Your subconscious mind determines all of these very important things about your life based on one simple standard: What it believes your current role is supposed to be. Or put another way, what it believes to be true, for you. Whatever it believes is true, for you, it will skillfully **make true** by feeding you impulses, ideas and feelings that dictate your moods and attitudes... which in turn determine your behavior, pursuits, interactions and ultimately the course of your life.

You tell your subconscious mind what role you're dedicated to playing, or what is true for you, in the language of **feelings**. It never doubts your feelings. It believes every one of them.

Your subconscious mind communicates back to you in feelings as well. In fact, you can know exactly what your subconscious mind believes to be true regarding each aspect of your life by thinking about any aspect of your life and then by paying attention to how you feel. Whatever you feel, happy or sad, positive or negative, is what your subconscious mind believes about that aspect of your life. And remember: Whatever it believes is true **it will make true**.

As an example, let's say you think about your social life and your subconscious mind believes you have a good social life. This being the case, you will immediately feel emotions of satisfaction, contentment and appreciation regarding your acquaintances, friends and loved ones. When you think of meeting new people, you'll experience feelings of excitement and anticipation. These impulses may prompt you to plan a party! If you feel good when you think about your social life, it's because your subconscious mind believes you're destined to have a satisfying social life and it will do everything necessary to make sure you do.

If on the other hand, you think about your social life and experience negative feelings such as loneliness, anxiety, inferiority or rejection, you can know that your subconscious mind believes you have a difficult time with people. When you think about meeting new people, you'll feel emotions that range from mild concern to paralyzing apprehension. These feelings may prompt you to decline the invitation to your coworker's party. Consciously, you might wish you had a better social life but you're not going to. Your subconscious mind will see to it that what it believes about your social life stays that way!

For your subconscious mind, it's all about congruency.

One thing your subconscious mind cannot endure is a gap between the reality it has created for you and what it believes that reality should be. If any of its beliefs regarding your role change, it must quickly change your reality and close that gap. It has no problem closing the gap once it decides to. It has all the tools necessary and will use them with skill and expertise. Never doubt this. One thing you can take to the bank is that whatever your subconscious mind believes is true about you is the way it's going to be! Period.

Now here's an interesting reality. Your subconscious mind doesn't care if your conscious mind is happy or sad, odd as this may sound. Your subconscious mind is simply a mechanism like a computer that can be programmed. Once programmed, it carries out that programing with exactness, whether your conscious mind enjoys the results or not. One explanation for this is that you grow and learn from all experience, both good and bad. All experience is valuable in the long run. You have to have a combination of both to grow. You'd quickly lose interest in your own life if everything were perfect all the time and there were never any challenges to work on. On the other hand, the more miserable you become the more determined you feel to make changes in your life.

So what can you do if your subconscious mind believes something about you that you don't like? How can you turn a negative subconscious belief into a positive one?

The answer is so simple that you'll wonder why you haven't understood it all along. Since your subconscious mind hears, obediently responds to and is programmed by feelings, all you have to do to reprogram a negative belief into a positive one is **stop feeling bad** about that aspect of your life and **start feeling good** about it!

Believe me, I know what you're thinking. You're thinking, "Wait a minute! How am I supposed to stop feeling bad about my social life, for example, and start feeling good about it if I don't have any friends and nobody likes me?" That's an excellent question. Let me answer it in the next chapter.

Notes

Notes

Three

The Greatest Gift

As a human being, you have a unique ability. You can create imaginary scenarios in your mind which generate intense feelings. You do it all the time.

Have you ever had an argument? When it was over, what did you do? Of course, you re-lived that argument over and over in your mind. You didn't just re-live what **actually** happened, you added and deleted things. You imagined saying things you didn't say before, probably very witty and clever things. As you imagined verbally overpowering your opponent and setting his or her thinking straight, you experienced intensely satisfying feelings of vindication and victory. Maybe you went so far as to imagine punching that person in the nose! If you did, you probably felt a deep sense of satisfaction mixed with feelings of grave concern regarding the consequences of taking such action. Those latter feelings are what keep you from punching everyone you disagree with.

Have you ever created a daydream about being in love? Maybe you imagined being with someone you already know or maybe your sweetheart was a complete figment of your imagination. Either way, you wandered off together in your mind, hand in hand, talking about things that are important to you and interacting in a sweet and tender way. As you did this, you experienced the intensely pleasurable feelings associated with being in love. You may have even felt excitement and anticipation as you leaned in for an imaginary kiss!

Now, as you create imaginary scenarios in your mind, you know they're not real, don't you? But what about the feelings they generate, are those real? Of course they are! Your subconscious mind hears and responds to all of your feelings regardless of whether they're generated by real life or in your imagination. It simply believes your feelings and makes constant, tiny adjustments to keep reality congruent with your predominant feelings.

Each one of your core subconscious beliefs was programmed by an intense feeling associated with an event or situation. Some of that programming took place outside of your control when you were a child. Some of your subconscious beliefs were programmed very much within your control, although you may not have been aware of exactly what you were doing at the time.

To illustrate how imaginary scenarios create feelings that affect your reality, let's consider two make-believe boys who I'll name Johnny and Jimmy.

Johnny and Jimmy play little league football and obviously, both of them want to do well. Johnny and Jimmy are almost identical in every way except one. When Johnny thinks of football, his head becomes filled with spectacular visions of grandeur! For significant moments throughout each day he creates exciting daydreams about football. He envisions himself taking a hand-off from the Quarterback. He fakes a cut to the inside then jukes to the outside. He stiff-arms a would-be tackler, spin-moves, turns on his speed and outruns everybody into the end zone. He scores! The crowd goes wild, clapping and cheering... inside Johnny's head.

Johnny runs these animated movies of success over and over in his mind and as he does, he generates intense feelings of excitement, peer acceptance and pure fun as it relates to football. All the while, his subconscious mind is listening to these feelings and believing them. It never doubts them for a second. So, the more Johnny creates these intensely fun, exciting and successful feelings, the more his subconscious mind believes that this is what Johnny's reality is supposed to look like. It then goes to work manipulating every situation and circumstance to make it true.

Now, Jimmy likes football too. However, he's a very practical boy and so quite naturally, he's concerned about getting hit too hard. Sometimes it hurts and if he's not careful he could even sustain an injury. He also worries about how long practice will run tonight and how hard it will be. Don't misunderstand, Jimmy likes football too and wants to succeed. He thinks about doing well sometimes but he spends **more time worrying** about things like running wind sprints or dropping a pass in front of the cheerleaders which would be very embarrassing. For significant moments throughout each day he dwells on these feelings of concern, worry and even dread

30

associated with football... **and his subconscious mind is listening!**

Who's going to be the better football player? Who is more likely to make a one-handed catch during practice, get noticed by the coach and subsequently get put on the first string? Of course, all other variables being equal, it's Johnny. He sees himself making that one-handed catch several times every day. More importantly he **feels** it! The exact one-handed catch Johnny imagines may or may not happen, **but other things will happen**, things that create feelings that match the feelings Johnny generates in his imagination. That's how it works!

At some point, Johnny may shift his focus away from football and start dreaming about being the world's greatest surgeon or business man. But for now, he's going to enjoy a successful little league football experience which will provide a foundation for even more success in his future.

Can you see why it's true when someone says, "If you think you can or think you can't, you're right!" It's even more accurate to say, "If you feel you can or feel you can't, you're right!"

Unfortunately, and due purely to a lack of understanding, you haven't always created happy and exciting scenarios in your mind. You may have spent substantial moments of time dwelling on negative things, even to the point of habitual negativity.

The quickest way to change your life is by **FLOODING** your subconscious mind with intensely positive feelings. Since dwelling on reality, if it's not what you want it to be, produces negative feelings, **STOP!** Instead, generate wildly exhilarating, compelling and uplifting imaginary scenarios and dwell on those!

To generate these wonderfully exciting imaginary scenarios, you'll use words, thoughts, pictures and even music but your subconscious mind is only interested in the feelings.

There's an old proverb that says, "If there is an attribute you desire to possess, act as if you already have it and soon it will be yours."

We have a word for this process. It's called **Pretending**. Pretending is simply acting as if you already have something you'd like to own, experience or be.

When you consciously identify a set of things you want and then pretend that you **already** have them, you immediately experience a portion of the same feelings you would enjoy if you **actually** had them.

As a child you were an absolute Pro at pretending! You could get into a make-believe world like nobody's business and stay there for hours! You'd pretend to have and be all kinds of wonderful things! As you did, you immersed yourself in the intensely pleasurable feelings associated with those things. That's why you did it. It felt good! It was fun! In those moments of childhood play, your subconscious mind obediently **listened** to and **believed** those feelings. Many of the core attributes and attitudes you now possess were programmed into your subconscious mind during those sessions of play and they have defined much of who you are and what you've experienced in life up to now.

However, not everything in your life has turned out like your sessions of childhood play. Why? Well, you stopped pretending that way. You were actually **taught** to stop pretending. Sometimes you were even scolded for doing it. You were told to get your head out of the clouds and focus on your homework. You were told to start living in the "real world." As you did, you bathed your subconscious mind in all the feelings of doing your homework, going to your job and living in the "real world." Over time your subconscious mind believed those feelings, as it always does, and went to work building a "real world" life to match.

Parts of your real world life are probably wonderful. Other parts may not be so great, but one thing is certain: You still possess the remarkable ability to pretend and that ability is eminently powerful. The ability to imagine and pretend is one of the greatest gifts God has given mankind.

This gift of imagination is responsible for everything that's ever been invented from a paper plate to your cell phone. Every invention began as a dream in someone's mind.

It's now time to go back to your childhood, dust off your ability to pretend and put it back to work... this time with maturity, purpose and intent.

When I read the interpretation of the metaphor of Sultan Musa of Mali's life I was shocked to find that many of the things he learned and wrote are paralleled in scripture that I was already familiar with. Two scriptures from the Bible line up perfectly with teachings found in Sultan Musa of Mali's interpretation.

"

"I tell you the truth, unless you change and become like little children, you will never enter the kingdom of heaven"

The New International Bible,
St. Matthew, chapter 18, verse 3

"

"nor will they say, 'See here!' or 'See there!' For indeed, the kingdom of God is within you."

The Bible, Luke chapter 17, verse 21

By identifying a specific set of invigorating and exciting attributes, places, things and situations you want to experience, and then pretending that you already have those things for significant moments each day, you can generate intense feelings of excitement, expectation, fun and success... and guess what? Your subconscious mind will be listening. If you persist in dwelling on exciting, motivating and exhilarating imaginings, permanent subconscious beliefs will form and your subconscious mind will then go to work closing the gap between these new beliefs and reality.

Pretending that things are, right now, exactly the way you'd like them to be is the most powerfully productive thing you can do to influence both your current level of happiness and your future.

You may think you don't have an imagination but it isn't true. Everybody has an imagination. Without one you wouldn't be able to decide what to wear in the morning or what to eat for breakfast. It is in your imagination that you know whether you like scrambled eggs or not. When you think of scrambled eggs you feel an impulse, good or bad toward eggs.

It's your imagination that makes you want to go on vacation. When you think of being away from work, sitting on a sandy beach sipping a cold, tropical drink with a loved one, you experience a portion of the pleasurable feelings associated with being on vacation. If this were not the case you'd never have the desire to go.

When you feel the impulses created by your imagination you are feeling the communication which is taking place between your conscious and subconscious minds. The goal of purposeful pretending is to take charge of this communication in a big and meaningful way.

A word of warning: Be careful not to confuse pretending with longing. They are not the same. Pretending is going into a state in which you actually see (in your mind's eye), experience and enjoy the things you want as if you have them right now. Longing is yearning for something you don't have and don't think you can have. Longing is a negative emotion. It makes you feel bad. It makes you vibrate on a low frequency. If you're longing for something, your subconscious mind hears and believes those feelings and responds by keeping what you want just out of reach.

Also, don't pretend with the goal of forcing reality to change. It doesn't work that way. Instead, dream up all kinds of fun and exciting possibilities and let those feelings fill your whole soul. As you go through life filled with intensely positive feelings, your physical reality will change. I'll prove this to you in chapter five.

Just focus on how you're feeling. If you're predominant feelings are exciting, successful, abundant, happy and positive, you're doing it right!

You have absolutely nothing to lose by doing this... nothing! And, you have everything to gain! There are no negative side effects associated with feeling positive, motivated and resourceful. You handle everything better when you feel this way... especially difficult challenges.

So, what do you know so far?

Secret One

You have two minds working simultaneously, a conscious mind and a subconscious mind. Your conscious mind dedicates itself to playing a specific role. Your subconscious mind sets the stage and keeps everything on it congruent with the role your subconscious mind thinks you're supposed to play. Your subconscious mind has all power and ability to set the stage you tell it to create.

Secret Two

Your subconscious mind hears, responds to and is programmed by feelings. It will keep your reality aligned with the predominant feelings you speak to it.

Secret Three

You have the ability to generate intense feelings by creating imaginary scenarios in your mind. You are free to choose what type of scenarios you dwell on. Whether you dwell on imaginary scenarios that feed your subconscious mind intensely positive or intensely negative feelings, your subconscious mind will hear and believe them.

Once a subconscious belief is formed, your subconscious mind goes to work with power and precision to make that belief true over time. It's now time to answer a simple but incredibly powerful question.

What do you want?

Notes

Four

A Simple Question

In the metaphor for his life, Aladdin and the Magic Lamp, Sultan Musa of Mali tells us that the Genie only says two things. The first is a question: "What is wanted?" The second is a statement: "Your wish is my command."

Your subconscious mind is always asking, "What do you want?" And, you're always answering by how you feel. Based on your feelings, your Genie fulfills your commands.

It's surprising to find how few people actually take the time to identify what it is they want.

Since pretending that things are, right now, the way you'd like them to be is the most powerfully productive thing you can do, it's vitally important to identify exactly how you'd like things to be.

What do you want?

If an all-powerful Genie appeared before you right now, and you knew you could instantly change anything in your life, what would you change and what would you change it to?

As you ask yourself this question, write down the answers.

When I work with clients whether in a one-on-one setting or a group workshop, I know that the most important step in their progression is to get them to identify what they really want and **write it down**. A lot of people struggle with this. It takes coaching to get most people to do the exercises, ask the questions and write down the answers. Why? Because their conscious minds are really good at doing what they're supposed to do, namely they're good at committing to and clinging to their current role.

Those who are new to these types of exercises tend to throw up obstacles. They immediately place restrictions on their desires. I have to remind them that this is their imagination. They can have it any way they want. No one can stop them from dreaming. It's all about finding your happy thoughts, those thoughts that elevate your mood and get you pumped up and excited.

Remember: That's the ultimate goal, to get pumped up and excited! When your mind is filled with exhilarating possibilities and you're sizzling with excitement, it flips the odds of success in your favor.

If you were to play a game of chance with a substantial amount of money on the line and you knew the odds were 70:30 against you, you might not be very excited about playing the game because you'd know that the longer you play the more you'll lose. However, if you could push a button and flip the odds to 70:30 in your favor, that would change everything. Now, the longer you play the more you win! When you're pumped up, excited, feeling energetic, happy and resourceful, you do better at everything. You've flipped the odds! The more you put yourself out there when you're feeling great, the more assuredly good things will come of your efforts.

If you could learn a handful of exercises that guarantee that the rest of your life is spent feeling powerful, positive and resourceful, then I could predict with total confidence that you'll have a successful and productive life. This is what Imagination Therapy is designed to do, to dramatically change your moods and attitudes which will change your focus, motivation, behavior and vibrational frequencies. People who play the game of Imagination Therapy on a consistent basis get results, often times stunning results!

Name Disclaimer: I call it "Imagination Therapy" but it is not clinical therapy and I'm not a therapist, just a coach. Imagination Therapy seemed like a fun name because it's the exact opposite of the popular term "Reality Therapy." Instead of focusing on reality, which can cause worry, concern and stress, I teach people to focus on fun and exciting imaginary scenarios, which makes them feel hopeful, expectant and motivated.

One of the first clients I worked with, a man I'll call Clint (name and minor details changed for privacy) had a lot of problems. He had poor health, his marriage was in trouble and he had very serious financial problems. Over the years, these issues had worn him out. He was extremely depressed, felt hopeless, spoke in a negative manner and even joked about suicide from time to time.

I asked Clint to play a game with me. I said, "Clint, if an all-powerful Genie appeared before you right now in a cloud of green smoke and asked you in a booming voice, "What do you want?!" How would you respond? What would you change?" Clint went blank. He couldn't tell me anything specific except to say, "I'd change everything."

This shocked me. I thought at very least he'd throw out a big number like "One million dollars!"

I pressed him. "What kind of car would you drive if you could have any car on the planet? You don't have to pay for it. It just falls out of the sky and it's yours. What car do you want?"

Clint thought a moment and answered. "A lime green Jeep Wrangler."

"Good." I said, "Now get in your Jeep and describe what you see, what you smell, what the engine sounds like when you fire it up." He did.

Then I said, "Now, back out of the driveway knowing that you're going to drive to your dream home. Again, you just have your dream home. Don't worry about how you got it... and as you drive up to your dream home describe it to me. Where is it? What style is it? What are the surroundings like?"

After a short pause he said, "It's a beautiful log style home in the mountains with a long driveway meandering through trees... and it's fall. All the leaves are changing colors."

As Clint did this I observed some physical changes in his posture, his breathing and the tempo of his speech. These few minutes of Imagination Therapy not only significantly improved his mood, but also his physicality.

We continued on this path until our time was up and then I gave him an assignment.

"Next time we get together, please bring written statements of roughly five things you'd love to have, be or do. For each statement, please bring an assortment of pictures that depict the things you'd love to experience and enjoy."

The next time he came, he had several sheets of paper with statements written on them and pictures he'd torn out of magazines which depicted the things he wanted to have pasted on them.

As he showed me the pictures and described what he wanted, I noticed him returning to the powerful, excited and positive mood he'd achieved the last time we talked. I asked him to notice the change, which he did. He told me that he had set aside fifteen minutes every night just before going to bed to look at his dream sheets, build his dream world all around him in his mind and then step into that world and enjoy it. He said that those fifteen minutes were the highlight of each day.

"That's wonderful!" I said, "But I'm going to ask you to flip the ratio. From now on, instead of going into your dream world for fifteen minutes a day... come out for fifteen minutes a day, if you want to."

Clint got it! Over the following weeks, he became obsessed with Imagination Therapy. He did it for significant moments each day, no matter what was going on in his "real world." He did this because it was fun! It made him feel good and he desperately needed to feel good. As he went through each day feeling pumped up and excited, crazy coincidences began to occur. One day, not many months into our sessions, Clint called me with some fantastic news. His brother had recommended him to be a Trustee for a real estate conglomerate. The trust was designed to shield assets from potential liability. It was a paid position and the starting salary was $4,000 per month. The extra money changed everything for Clint! Over time, he got involved in more of the same type of deals and his income continued to grow.

Today, Clint is doing amazingly well. Not only did his finances improve dramatically but his health improved as well. He and his wife are in love like school kids. His children, who were really struggling, are all doing very, very well. He's surrounded himself with vehicles, toys, experiences and other things that make him really happy... and he would never dream of suicide in his current situation.

So how about you? What do you want? If an all-powerful Genie appeared before you right now, would you know what your heart really desires? What would fulfill your deep, inner needs? Or would you tell the Genie to create what you think you're supposed to want or what others have told you to want? What areas of your life would you change and what would you change them to? Take a few minutes to answer the following questions.

Is there anything you can think of that if it were to happen would get you sizzling with excitement?

Where would you live if you could live anywhere in the world?

If you could have a second home anywhere in the world, where would it be?

What would you drive? What color would it be?

What toys would you own?

Who would you be with, and how would that person treat you?

What would you do for work if you could do anything you wanted?

How much money would you make? How would you spend it? How would you invest it?

How would you look? How would you feel?

How would family members, loved ones, friends, neighbors, business associates and even strangers benefit by having you around?

As you answer these questions, you will eventually find a handful of answers that not only get you pumped up and excited but also seem fairly plausible. Write these answers down as statements in the present tense. For example, "I live in Hawaii!" Then go to Google Images and collect pictures that support the feelings these thoughts and statements give you. Pictures are worth a thousand words. They're very powerful for generating the feelings necessary to program the subconscious mind. Next, make exciting dream sheets with statements and pictures regarding the aspects of your life you want to improve. Put these sheets in plastic page-protectors and then put the page-protectors in a three ring binder. Then imagine and pretend to your heart's content!

Your dream sheets can and should change as time goes on. In fact, it's rare that I don't fine tune one of my statements or add or delete at least one picture on my dream sheets every couple of days.

There are roughly eight aspects of life.

1. Health and fitness

2. Career and finances

3. Romantic relationship

4. Family and friends

5. Homes and cars

6. Fun and recreation

7. Spirituality and religion

8. Community and service

You don't need a hundred happy thoughts... just find three to five incredibly powerful ones. By focusing on these powerful happy thoughts, you'll instantly elevate your mood in a way that will alter and benefit all aspects of your life.

It's a fact that your subconscious mind is currently programmed with all kinds of limiting beliefs. Those limitations will pop up and remind you of your current reality when you try to pretend things are otherwise. For those people with conscious minds that are especially gifted at dedicating themselves to a role and clinging to it, it can be very difficult to let go of reality long enough to dream up and believe in a different life... a dream life. Luckily, Musa was taught something by the man made of light that makes it much easier to do. Once you understand the next secret, Secret Five, you'll be able to easily sweep away limiting beliefs because you'll understand that what you previously thought of as the "real world" is not the world with the power. There is another world, one you have near complete control over and it is this world that controls your physical world and determines your future.

In the next chapter, I'll teach you a new word, one you've never heard before, unless you heard it directly or indirectly from me or someone else with first-hand knowledge of Sultan Musa of Mali's texts. Once you fully grasp the meaning of this word and the secret associated with it, you'll be in a position to instigate massive and meaningful change in your life.

This is what you know up to this point:

Secret One

Your subconscious mind is in charge. It has the power to mold and shape your life into what it believes it's supposed to be.

Secret Two

By speaking the language of feelings, you have the ability to tell your subconscious mind exactly what to believe.

Secret Three

By pretending that things are exactly the way you want them to be, you can generate intensely exciting, happy and successful feelings. If done consistently, your subconscious mind becomes reprogrammed to create an exciting, happy and successful life.

Secret Four

By answering the question, "What is wanted?"
and identifying three to five extremely powerful
"happy thoughts" and by writing them down and
supporting them with pictures, you can pretend with
enough purpose, intensity and consistency to get results.

Notes

Five

The
"Real World"
Redefined

Up to this point, we've covered four very simple concepts regarding the way your subconscious mind works and how it can be consciously programmed with beliefs that produce much happier, more satisfying experiences. Now I'm going to give you some real meat. Secret Five is heavier than the others but it's the trick that makes it all work.

There's a possibility that what I'm about to tell you will conflict with your religious beliefs or lack of them. If this happens, please try to accept this concept as simply a valuable mental exercise. If you'll apply the concept, you'll get results. The results validate the concept, irrespective of the source. Here's what I mean by that. If you were to take a human relations course and the professor referred to the Golden Rule, which is: "Do unto others as you would have others do unto you," you might recognize that quote as coming from the Bible. You may have a positive reaction or you may have a negative reaction and say, "I'm not into religion." The concept however, is a very effective human relations concept. If you put it into practice, you'll do better with people. You don't have to accept the source to apply the concept. If it works, it works!

Secret Five was taught to Musa when he had an out-of-body experience in the cave.

Musa was taught that everyone has a physical body and a spirit body. The spirit body resides in and around the physical body. This spirit body is a very real body made of very real spirit molecules...

and it is the spirit body that has the life! This is the body that matters the most.

The only evidence I'll offer to back up this concept of a spirit body, for now, is the phenomenon of death. If the physical body becomes uninhabitable due to injury or disease, the spirit body leaves, literally ejecting itself from the physical. When this happens, the physical body becomes a lifeless, inanimate lump of tissue. It becomes dead. You can poke it with a pin and it feels nothing. It's your spirit body that animates the physical body. It's your spirit body that feels. **It's your spirit body that is the real you!**

If you've studied basic physics, you already know that nothing is truly solid. Everything, including the chair you're sitting on or the concrete curbing along the side of the road is made of tiny molecules that vibrate on particular frequencies. These molecules have a positive and a negative charge. They are attracted to and adhere to each other magnetically.

Just as your physical body is made of real, physical molecules, your spirit body is made of real molecules too, just different molecules. Spirit molecules are infinitely superior in their composition. They are of a higher quality, finer and incorruptible. And while formations made of spirit material are not typically visible to the physical eye, it is real material nonetheless... and this material is alive!

In and around every physical formation is a spirit formation. This may be a lot to digest but I'm going to keep moving. You'll absorb more as we go. Also, it may sound like I'm being repetitive. This is done on purpose. When trying to change a belief, repetition is your best friend!

Spirit molecules, which are alive, respond obediently to vibrations generated by human feelings.

By generating intensely exciting imaginary scenarios in your mind, you can generate strong feelings (vibrations) that powerfully impact, ply and mold spirit molecules and material. With the power of your mind, you can alter existing spirit formations as well as create entirely new ones and you can do this rather easily and quickly.

Creative people like architects, musicians, artists and inventors typically understand that everything is created in the mind first, before it's created physically, even if they don't understand the real science behind this concept. The reality is that when people create in their minds, **they are actually manipulating spirit molecules into spirit things.**

Spirit molecules can be organized into spirit forms lightning fast and with relative ease by using your imagination. When you imagine something with a certain level of intensity and belief, to the point where you actually see it in your mind's eye and feel it in your spirit, you have successfully organized spirit molecules into that form... it is a real thing! Now, if you let go of that imagery and don't build it again, those spirit molecules will dissipate into the wind, as it were, and become available to be used later. However, if you hold onto that image and revisit it often, at some point it becomes permanent. Once it becomes a permanent spirit formation it immediately exerts magnetic force on the physical realm.

The study and understanding of the laws that govern the physical world is called Physics. The study and understanding of the laws that govern the spirit world is called **SPYRICS**. This is the new word I promised to teach you.

Now here's the fun part of Spyrics: Physical molecules are magnetically attracted to spirit molecules. When a new, permanent spirit form is created, powerful gravitational force is applied to the physical realm. In other words, permanent spirit formations or constructs *want* to become physical constructs and begin exerting magnetic force on the world to make it happen. It can take a period of time for a permanent spirit construct to become physical but unless the spirit form is dispersed, its physical creation *will* occur. (Sometimes [but not always], this physical creation is not the exact form of what you imagine but it matches the feelings or frequencies of what you imagine. This is a phenomenon that I won't take the time to cover in detail in this book, but I do cover it in workshops.)

This physical change often involves human exertion (work and activity), but that exertion takes place naturally and efficiently because of the impulses, feelings and motivations generated by the spirit formation itself.

As an illustration of this fact, I want to tell you the following story. One day I sat down with my brother and a close family friend to watch a video documentary that featured, in part, a man who participated in a famous twelve week fitness challenge. This man took pictures of himself before and after the challenge. He held a newspaper in the photographs to document the time period.

In his before pictures, he was completely out of shape. He had a little round belly and a chubby, round, undefined face.

Within three months he transformed his physical appearance so dramatically that the company hosting the challenge included him in the video documentary. In the documentary this man explained that he had found a picture of a famous body builder. Every morning and several times throughout each day, he studied the picture and imagined himself looking exactly like the body builder. He pretended to be the man in the picture.

As he pretended to be that man, something astonishing happened! In those moments of intense pretending, he experienced over-powering motivational impulses to **act** like he imagined the famous body builder would act. When you have an amazing body that you're proud of, you don't stuff it with donuts or soda pop! You don't ride the elevator either. You run up the stairs every chance you get. You work out in the gym ferociously every day and make other healthy choices, such as eating a meticulous diet and getting plenty of regenerative sleep. This man took pride in supporting his body through these types of choices.

In the beginning, he pictured himself looking exactly like the famous body builder for several seconds at a time, three or four times a day. As time went on, he was able to pretend much more often and for longer periods of time. With each intense workout and other activity that supported this new image of himself, his ability to pretend intensified. Soon, he was pretending with such intensity and consistency that he came to totally believe that he looked like the body builder, long before his physical body had made much of a transformation. In fact, there was a period of time when he would see a reflection of himself in a mirror or window, and be shocked that he didn't look like the body builder. In these moments, he would willfully ignore the physical shape of his body and go right back to pretending to have the body he desired... and taking care of it accordingly. He actually began to avoid mirrors for a period of time because he didn't want anything to limit his ability to imagine and believe.

Within three months of **acting** like a man with an amazing physique, his body had made a remarkable transformation! He looked almost identical to the famous body builder in the photograph. As we saw the before and after pictures, we were truly amazed and inspired. But there was something else very strange. We all noticed it at about the same time. Each of us exclaimed in unison, "Wow, look at his face!" Even his face had changed to resemble the famous body builder! It stood to reason that pretending to have a perfect body would generate the motivation to eat right and work out aggressively and that over time his body would respond, but what exercise did he do to cause his face to look like the body builder?

You already know that your physical body is always in a state of change, right? You don't look like you did ten years ago and ten years ago you didn't look like you did as a baby. Ten years from now you won't look like you do today. You also know that it's possible to exert influence on the form and appearance of your physical body. For example, with the right type of diet and exercise you can change, even dramatically, the way your physical body looks. The amount of time it takes for these physical changes to occur is linked to the amount of effort you exert. The effort you exert is linked to the feelings of desire, enthusiasm, motivation and commitment you feel in your spirit. These feelings are linked to the images and scenarios you choose to entertain in your mind.

Your spirit body is completely different from your physical body in that you can change its form and appearance instantly and with very little effort. Let me repeat that. You can change the actual form of your very real spirit body almost instantaneously, just like the man in the twelve week challenge. Your spirit is a shapeshifter! When you envision your body a certain way with a certain amount of belief and intensity, the actual spirit form of your body changes shape to emulate the image you're holding in your mind. When this happens, you can *feel* what it's like to have this new form or in other words, to be this new person.

If you quit pretending, your spirit body will instantly snap back to the way it was but while you're pretending, your spirit body (which remember is a real body) is **really** in the form you're imagining. That's why you can feel the emotions associated with that form. This works with attributes as well as appearance.

When you imagine with intensity and belief that you are a strong, capable and bold person who can handle any situation, you **really** are, in spirit! In that moment, the molecular structure of your spirit body changes and maintains that form until you quit pretending.

But, what happens if you **don't** quit pretending? Let's say you consciously view yourself as a strong, capable and bold person consistently for substantial moments each day for an extended period of time, what then? Well, at some point your subconscious mind becomes so familiar with this new spirit form that it believes it. If you persist in viewing yourself this way, your subconscious mind will eventually believe this new form is your true form because you have quit viewing yourself any other way. At this point your spirit quits snapping back. From that moment on, your subconscious mind has been reprogrammed to believe that you are a strong, capable and bold person who can handle any situation. Once your subconscious mind believes this to be true, it goes into action, powerfully gravitating to this situation and avoiding that one, attracting this person and repelling that one, creating all of the events and circumstances necessary to make this new subconscious belief or spirit form true in your physical world as well.

Not only do you have the power to quickly manipulate the form and appearance of your spirit body, but you have the power to easily reorganize the spirit formation of anything and everything in your life. Of course you have to operate within certain boundaries but those boundaries are much wider than most people have any idea.

Since physical molecules are magnetically attracted to spirit molecules, they obediently reorganize themselves, over time, to mimic spirit forms.

Let's engage in a little exercise that will make this concept easier to grasp.

Take a moment to imagine your tummy the way you would like it to be. No matter your current physical condition, just use your imagination to see your tummy as you'd like it to be. **Don't put any restrictions on this.** This is your imagination. You can have it any way you want. If you'd like a six pack of rippling muscle, envision that. If you just want a flat, toned tummy, picture it that way. There's no wrong way to imagine your tummy for the purpose of this exercise, just make sure that for at least a few seconds you get to the point where you can imagine your tummy the way you'd like it to be until you feel it as though it's real. Don't stop envisioning until you've achieved that vision and feeling. Ready? Go!

Okay. Did you get to where you could see it in your mind? Could you feel it as though it were real for at least a second or two? If you did, did you notice any physical changes taking place? Did you sit or stand any taller? Did you suck in your tummy or tighten your muscles at all? Did you experience any physical changes, however small, while doing this mental exercise? Of course you did! Changing the form of your spirit body induces change in your physical body.

If having a perfectly toned tummy turns you on and if you persist in viewing yourself this way with belief, intensity and consistency, the positive feelings associated with having a great looking set of abs would motivate you to action. You'd eat and exercise a little differently. At first the changes might be subtle and seem almost insignificant but over time these changes build on each other and develop into full measure, changing the circumstances and trajectory of your life. Weird things may happen such as "coincidentally" running into someone who has a great set of abs and is more than happy to teach and motivate you along the way to achieving the abs of your dreams. These "coincidences" will be orchestrated by your subconscious mind. You don't really have to worry about how the results will be achieved. All you have to do is permanently change the spirit form of your abs and commit to act on the new feelings and impulses this new form provokes.

While we're on the topic of physical work and exertion, it's important to understand that physical work is a byproduct of spiritual work.

Consistently dwelling on extraordinarily exciting thoughts and images triggers impulses that propel us to action. The man in the documentary didn't just sit around pretending to be in great shape and then wake up one morning with an amazing body. **As he pretended to have an amazing body, he experienced the powerfully rewarding and subsequently** motivating feelings associated with that experience. Those subtle but powerful feelings drove him to act. That action filled him with a sense of hope, purpose and pride. Everything he did to support his dream of having an exceptionally fit body was exciting, productive and uplifting! In those moments, he was literally living the life of his dreams... the life of a man with an amazing body and he loved every minute of that lifestyle.

He enjoyed a portion of the intensely pleasurable feelings associated with having an amazing body the very moment he pretended with intensity and belief to have such a body and then he enjoyed even more pleasurable feelings three months later when that body was a physical reality. Once he created a tremendously fit spirit body and made it permanent with persistent pretending, the change to his physical body was inevitable! That's how it works!

The same thing that was done with his body can be done with your body or any other aspect of your life. The idea of creating a body builder's physique may or may not be the thing that turns you on but something does! The trick is to find that something.

By identifying those thoughts and dreams that ignite your enthusiasm and fill your soul with red-hot excitement and by holding those compelling thoughts and dreams in your imagination with intensity, belief and consistency, you can change the spirit constitution of your world almost immediately. Once you reconstruct your spirit world everything changes, you change! You'll experience different feelings, impulses, ideas, desires and motivations and they'll, very naturally, dictate different behavior which will produce different results.

Almost all of the frustration you've experienced up to now stems from trying to do it the other way around. Trying to change physical realities without first changing spiritual realities is ineffectual.

If you see yourself as physically unfit and out of shape, you can go into the gym and do a few half-hearted reps on a couple machines but you won't have the motivation necessary to exert yourself with passion and purpose like the man in the story.

Likewise, if you see yourself as chronically poor, opportunity can be all around you but you won't see it or pursue it. To create drastic physical change, you have to first create drastic spiritual change.

Most people are waiting for something to change in their physical world so they can finally be happy. The truth is, you have to do the exact opposite! Get excited and happy first and then things will change in your physical world.

Your spirit is a powerful, magnetized transmitter and receiver. It exerts magnetic force on the physical world, either a lot or a little depending on the frequencies it is vibrating on. Since you are in control of the amount and intensity of the force you exert on the world, you are in almost complete control of your life. I say "almost" because you are here to act and to be acted upon. You obviously live within the parameters of a pre-designed, macro-construct but you have tremendous power and agency within this construct to manipulate and create the circumstances of your own life. There are things that you have experienced and will experience that you didn't create... things that were created by others exerting their will on the world. But you are in complete control of your response to these things.

Imagination is the key to reality.

Whether you are religious or not there's something to be learned by reading the account of the creation of the world found in the first chapter of Genesis in the Bible. Contrary to common belief, this account is NOT a description of the **physical** creation. It is a description of the **spiritual** creation only. This is made clear in the very next chapter, chapter two, verses four and five. These verses read, "This is the account of the heavens and of the earth when they were created, in the day that the Lord God created the earth and the heavens and every plant of the field **BEFORE** it was in the earth, and every herb of the field **BEFORE** it grew."

Like an architect setting aside one week to dream up and sketch a beautiful home or building, this account depicts a superior being using his imagination to design and create spirit forms. Every detail, every living plant and creature was envisioned with such clarity and intensity that each spirit construct was made permanent. These spirit constructs existed long before the physical world took form and like any construction project, when the physical creation took place, it followed the plan or blueprint that had been previously designed and created in spirit.

This account offers an invaluable clue for those who desire to take charge of their own lives and create their own future. Everything is created in spirit form before it is created physically.

Whether you regard yourself as a child of God or not, one thing is inarguable: you have the ability to create. You do it every day. Whether you create a bowl of cereal with milk poured over it and a spoon stuck into it ready to eat, or you're working on an invention that will change the world... all creation starts with envisioning what it is you want to do. I refer to this process as Creation Thinking. So, why not make your creative thoughts remarkable, exciting and grand? No one can stop you from creating your dream world just the way you want it to be. And you have nothing to lose by doing it. You can only lose by not doing it.

To master Creation Thinking, you need only change your focus. Instead of focusing primarily on your physical world and allowing reality to get you down and depressed, build an amazing, exciting and awe-inspiring spirit world all around you and focus primarily on that world. As you do, you will be filled with vitality, hope and a sense of overwhelming fun.

> 66
>
> *"For to be carnally minded is death; but to be spiritually minded is life and peace..."*

The Bible, Romans chapter 8, verse 6

At this point it is reasonable to ask, "If I do this, how long will it take to achieve results?" Let me answer that question right now!

Notes

Six

Instant Success

It happens quite often when I'm speaking on this topic, either one-on-one with a client or in a workshop setting, or speaking to a large group of people that someone asks, "Okay Jeff, if I really do this... how long will it take to work?" I always answer, "If you're doing it right, it should work almost instantly!" Invariably they look at me like I misunderstood the question, and I teach them Secret Six.

Carefully consider this important question. Why do you want nice things? Why do you want a successful career or a nice car or beautiful home? Why do you want to be healthy and fit? Why do you want to be attractive and interesting? Why do you want great friends or the perfect sweetheart or plenty of money? The answer is, those things make you **FEEL GOOD!**

Feeling good is the primary goal of life and I'm not just talking about fun feelings either. Feeling courageous, loyal, dependable, honorable and strong in the face of challenges are also good feelings. If you feel good about your life, no matter what stage of life you're currently in, you're succeeding. If you feel bad about your life, you're failing. Since good feelings create good circumstances, it's reasonable to suggest that the very instant you take control of what you dwell on in your mind in such a way that you feel almost nothing but positive and successful feelings, you are a success! That spiritual success will inevitably attract the physical trappings of success.

To illustrate this, let's say that one of the nice things you want is a specific new car.

Take a moment and picture that car in your mind. Don't spend too much time choosing the type of car, just pick any car that would be really fun to own. If cars don't turn you on you can pick something else and do this exercise in the same basic way.

Now let's say you actually own that car free and clear. It doesn't matter how you got it, this is your imagination. The car is yours and it's sitting in front of your residence. Here's a question: What if you really own that car but you are in the kitchen and your car is outside in the driveway where you can't see or touch it, do you still have that car? Does it still feel good to own it? Of course you do and of course it does!

The fact is, the feelings you experience when you imagine, remember, or in any way think about your dream car are nearly identical to the feelings you'd have if you were in or near that car in "real life." You can give yourself the feelings of owning the car of your dreams right now. You can enjoy the feeling of having anything you want **RIGHT NOW**, simply by pretending to have it, by saying you have it, by remembering it and by imagining yourself enjoying it. You don't have to wait until you're physically in the car of your dreams to enjoy it. The minute you generate the dream of owning a great car, you have succeeded at the primary goal, which is to vibrate on the higher and more excited frequency of owning a really cool car.

Now of course, it's important to enjoy things physically. You can't physically pick up your date in a spirit car. However the quickest way to physically acquire the car of your dreams, if you make that one of your goals, is to create and persistently enjoy that car in your imagination. The programming that takes place during this process is incredibly powerful. Once your subconscious mind believes your dream car is supposed to be part of your life, it immediately feeds you powerful new ideas, motivation and impulses that lead to action. It also goes to work manipulating situations and circumstances that manifest as odd coincidences to make that car part of your physical reality.

Let me tell you a quick story to illustrate this point. I've always wanted to own a Land Rover Defender 110. They're the old safari-looking vehicles you see in movies filmed in Africa. Land Rover doesn't make the old Defender anymore and they're hard to come by. They're usually very expensive too, especially if they're in the United States. Several years ago I wrote down in my Dream Book that I own a green Defender 110. I also downloaded a bunch of pictures of green Defenders from Google Images and put them in my dream book. Now, I own several newer model Land Rovers which I and my family drive on a daily basis, so I didn't make owning a Defender an urgent goal. I just liked pretending to have one. I'd stared at those pictures and pretended to own a Land Rover Defender for over a year when one day, while visiting my farm in Belize, I noticed a green Defender parked in someone's front yard. On a whim I pulled in and asked the owner if he'd sell it. "Yes," he said, "For twenty thousand U.S." Now, that's about half what the same vehicle would cost in the States and even though it was a great price, I thought, "Okay, maybe I'll buy it in the near future but I'm not really ready to buy it now." Then I continued north to my place near Corozal Town. For the rest of the trip, as I drove around in the rental truck, I pretended to drive that green Defender.

On the way to the airport at the end of my trip, I pulled into the gas station to fill up the rental truck and there was the green Land Rover! The owner came over to greet me. He asked if I still wanted the Defender and I said, "Maybe someday but not right now." He said, "What if I make you the best deal in the world? I've got to take my family to Guatemala in three months and I need cash." I shook my head "No" but the words that came out of my mouth were, "What's the minimum amount you'd take for it?" He said, "Twelve thousand." At that price, I simply couldn't pass it up. We shook hands and the next time I came to Belize, about two months later, I brought him the cash and took my green Land Rover Defender 110 to my farm. I absolutely love owning that Defender! It makes me all giddy and warm when I think about it, even when I'm in the States and it's clear over in Belize.

You can create anything you want, spiritually speaking, and give it to yourself right now! There's nothing you can't have, nothing you can't experience. Nothing is outside of your reach. Once you've created exciting things in your imagination they become very real spiritual things and they take on a life of their own. They want to become physical realities and they exert magnetic force on the physical world to make it happen. Your subconscious mind responds to this magnetic force, if it is strong enough and manipulates situations and circumstances to make spiritual things become physical realities. Your conscious mind sees these manipulations as strange coincidences but they're all orchestrated by your subconscious mind.

You don't have to wait for something extraordinary to happen in your external world to experience a fun, exciting and successful life. In fact, it's the other way around. You have to first experience an exhilarating, fun life spiritually and then extraordinary things begin to happen in your physical world!

There are laws in place that regulate which spirit creations become physical constructs and which ones remain in the realm of fantasy. If this were not the case, you wouldn't be able to enjoy your imagination. You wouldn't be able to experience make-believe scenarios without each one becoming real in the physical world. Every time you imagined owning a new car it would appear. You'd have so many cars piled up in your driveway that you wouldn't be able to get to your home, I mean homes. It would be quite a mess!

Thankfully, you can enjoy all kinds of things in your imagination without physically creating them. This means that you have an unlimited opportunity to experience, explore and enjoy life! You can employ the skill of pretending as often as you desire and experience all kinds of fantastic situations and circumstances with their accompanying enjoyable feelings. This is what having a rich, abundant and full life is about. In addition, you will be able to select a special set of spirit formations to create in the physical realm. These things will be objects, experiences, situations and circumstances that bring you immense joy, excitement and fulfillment and fit into the realities, values and goals associated with your physical life. This set of things will be unique to you. It may actually surprise you when you find out what you really want as opposed to what you currently think you want, or have been told to want.

Once this set of deeply personal, exciting and compelling dreams has been identified and created in spirit form, you'll be able to naturally and easily commit your life's efforts to creating it physically.

When I was a young boy, a famous adventurer came to talk to our Scout Troop. He showed pictures of wonderful places and told us heart-pounding stories of exciting and often dangerous expeditions he'd been on. He seemed so happy, excited and full of life! This made an impression on me and I thought, "I want to live an exciting life too!"

Over the years I've thought about him and wondered, at what actual point in time did he become a great adventurer? Was it only at the end of a particularly successful expedition? The answer came back: "No." He was a great adventurer during the planning stages of his first expedition. He was a great adventurer during each expedition. He was even a great adventurer when an expedition didn't go as planned. In actuality, he became a great adventurer the very moment he created a believable and exciting vision of himself as an adventurer and then committed himself to that vision by persistently pretending to be that man and playing that role.

The point is this: To begin living the life of your dreams, all you have to do is create the dream and then step into that dream-world and stay there. You can persistently pretend to be the person you want to be, right now. You don't have to wait.

Do you want to be the CEO of a highly profitable company? Create that dream and experience that role in your imagination now! Do you want to be a famous performer, a terrific husband and father, or wife and mother? Do you want to be a healer, a dancer or a teacher? Create and enjoy those experiences now! Do you want to be physically fit, healthy, smart, sexy, wealthy and wise? Do you want to travel to exotic places or even live in one? Give those experiences to yourself right now!

As you create intensely exciting dreams of who you are and what you want to have and experience, the composition of your spirit body and spirit world will change. You will immediately experience a portion of the good feelings and impulses associated with those dreams and it will feel great! Feeling great is the primary goal. Feeling great is just another way of saying that your spirit is vibrating on highly successful frequencies. When you consistently vibrate on the frequencies of success, you are a success! The physical counterparts of success will surely follow. Once you've changed the way you envision yourself, you've actually changed who you are.

This is what you know up to this point:

Secret One

Your subconscious mind is in charge.

Secret Two

Your subconscious mind hears, responds to and is programmed by feelings.

Secret Three

You can generate intensely positive feelings by employing the skill of pretending.

Secret Four

Answering the question, "What is wanted?" allows you to pretend with power and purpose.

Secret Five

You can quickly redesign and rebuild your spirit world. Your spirit world exerts irresistible, magnetic force on your physical world.

Secret Six

Because you act on your feelings, when you consistently produce successful feelings, you will act in a successful manner. When you consistently act in a successful manner you are a success, right now! As morning follows night, the physical trappings of success follow right behind spiritual success.

Notes

Notes

Notes

Seven

The Art
of Receiving

To Musa's great relief and joy, he learned that a force exists, and has existed since the beginning of creation, which can be harnessed and used by mankind to create. Musa was taught exactly how to harness this force.

This force for creation has been spoken of in every ancient spiritual text since the beginning of recorded history. This force has a name and that name is **FAITH**.

Faith as a force for creation is often misunderstood. To start with, faith is thought of as something you either have or don't have, but faith is something you **do** and then you have it.

Faith is done in your imagination. For example, when someone says they have faith in God, what they're really saying is they've chosen to imagine that an all-powerful being who loves and watches over them exists. A person who doesn't have faith in God has simply *chosen* **not** to imagine that.

Regardless of your faith or lack of faith in the existence of God, you know that faith as a force of creation exists. You've seen it in action. Every creation begins in somebody's imagination. If that person's dream is compelling enough, it turns into a plan and eventually it becomes a real physical thing. So, let's take a closer look at the concept of faith as a force for creation.

"... If ye have faith as a grain of mustard seed, ye shall say unto this mountain, Remove hence to yonder place; and it shall remove; and nothing shall be impossible unto you."

The Bible St. Matthew, chapter 17 verse 20

It's a common belief that this quote is referring to a quantity of faith, the idea being that there is a certain amount or quantity of faith needed to create and it isn't much, just the amount of a tiny mustard seed. But let's examine it in the light of what you now know. When you create exciting images in your mind, those images generate exciting feelings! Those feelings generate ideas, impulses and motivation, which in turn influence your behavior. Different behavior, no matter how subtle, produces different results.

In addition, when you feel excited, the molecules of your body vibrate on different frequencies which magnetically draw into your life circumstances, people and opportunities that vibrate on matching frequencies. With this in mind, it becomes clear that the images you entertain in your mind are similar to a grain of mustard seed in that **they are both seeds!** What do mustard seeds do? They eventually grow into mustard trees. What do exciting thoughts do? They eventually grow into exciting things.

The type of seeds you plant dictates what grows. When you plant exciting images in your mind, they turn into exciting situations! If you plant sorrowful seeds, they will grow into unhappy situations.

Because you have an unlimited ability to think exciting thoughts and imagine exciting scenarios, you have an unlimited ability to plant seeds of creation! Knowing that the images and scenarios you entertain in your mind grow like seeds into corresponding physical things, you'll want to plant as many positive and exciting seeds as you possibly can and avoid planting negative seeds all together!

"Be not deceived: God is not mocked: for whatsoever a man soweth, that shall he also reap."

The Bible, Galatians, chapter 6, verse 7

If I were to translate this verse into today's vernacular I'd say: "Don't kid yourself; natural law cannot be circumvented. The things you choose to dwell on in your mind, whether positive or negative, will have a profound and corresponding effect on your future."

IMAGINATION IS THE KEY TO REALITY!

Now I'm going to share with you the final secret that Musa learned. This secret allowed him to master the force of creation we refer to as faith. This secret is a formula. It is the formula Musa used to go from dirt poor street urchin to unbelievably wealthy merchant and eventually Sultan of the entire Mali Kingdom.

I refer to this formula as the C.A.R.T. Wheel. That's my name for the four phase formula which Sultan Musa of Mali described. I came up with this name to help me remember the four phases of the art of receiving.

1. Create. The first phase of the formula is what we've been talking about throughout this book. After you've identified the things that really turn you on, create them in your imagination until you can see them in your mind's eye and feel them in your spirit. Then...

2. Ask. With the thing you want created in your mind, ask for it in prayer. Asking puts you in the attitude of humility. You are at your most powerful when you're humble. Humility means that you recognize that you did not create your body or your mind. Those were given to you as gifts. You did not create the air you breathe or the water you drink. Those are gifts as well. When you realize how many wonderful gifts you've already received, it's easier to believe in receiving more.

If, for example, you're dealing with a specific health problem and you think, "It would take a miracle to get healthy again," but you imagine that miracle taking place and ask for it, you'll likely realize that everything about you is a miracle! It's a miracle that you can see with your eyes, talk with your mouth and move about on your legs and feet. In this attitude of recognizing the miracles you've already experienced, it's easier to believe in one more miracle taking place.

It also takes humility to ask for what you really want... to be honest about what you want.

Asking in faith is a principle with a promise.

> *"And all things, whatsoever ye shall ask in prayer, believing, ye shall receive."*

The Bible, Mattew, chapter 21, verse 22

The word "believing" in this quote is like the concept of faith. You can either **do** believing or not do it and the only way to do it is in your imagination. When you ask for what you want, while holding the spirit creation of that thing in your mind as though you already have it, and continue holding it after you ask, you're doing it right... you're asking in faith, believing.

3. Receive. Use your imagination to receive the gift. I do this by inventing mental exercises for myself and for my clients. Earlier, I told you about Clint with his very serious financial problems. Together, we came up with an exercise for Clint to perform during prayer (and at other times during the day). When he got to phase three, he would imagine receiving the gift he was asking for, the gift of more money, by looking slightly upward with his hands out, palms up, and imagine

$100 bills falling from the sky. This mental exercise broke the spell of the negative belief his subconscious mind once held that money was hard to come by and it bolstered Clint's ability to believe that the blessing of more money could come to him.

4. Thanks. Phase four is summed up in the following phrase from the Sultan's text. I can only share the sentiment from memory. However, I've since found a scripture that expresses the Sultan's phrase perfectly, including the multiplier of one hundred.

"And he who receiveth all things with thankfulness shall be made glorious; and the things of this earth shall be added unto him, even an hundred fold, ye, more."

The Doctrine and Covenants, section 78, verse 19

Being thankful is a little different than being grateful. Being thankful is feeling grateful and then opening your mouth and expressing it. There is tremendous power in expressing thanks for the things you receive.

Thankfulness is a principle with a promise too. When you're thankful for the things you receive, more of what you want is drawn into your life. You can put it to the test and see the results with your own eyes. If you're having trouble with an employee, a spouse, child, friend, neighbor or anyone else, try thanking them sincerely for anything and everything they do right and watch what happens. Be subtle and smart. Start off small and increase the instances of thanking them over time. There is no better way to transform a bad relationship.

If you're having trouble in any area of your life, take finances for example, try offering thanks for every dollar that has ever come to you and for every dollar that will come to you in the future. Say thanks often and keep a record of what happens.

Thankfulness puts you on the frequency to receive. When you come to understand and practice thankfulness, you will see the things of this earth, the things you want, rush into your life with much more ease and speed.

A word of warning. When there are a lot of things we need and want, it's natural to feel like things aren't coming to us fast enough. When this happens, we tend to allow our happiness and excitement to slip away and we become impatient instead. Watch out for impatience. Impatience is a negative emotion. It is contrary to faith. It gums up the works and can slow down or even stop the process of receiving. The cure for impatience is thankfulness. Stay in your beautiful, fun and exciting dream-world and offer thanks for everything in it. Act on the promptings your dream-world gives you. Do the things the person of your dreams would do and have faith. As you live each moment in a spiritually successful state, the physical counterparts of that success will come.

You've now learned each of the Sultan's Seven Secrets:

Secret One

Your subconscious mind is in charge.

Secret Two

Secret Three

Your subconscious mind hears, responds to and is programmed by feelings.

You can generate intensely positive feelings by pretending.

Secret Four

Answering the question, "What is wanted?" allows you to pretend with power and purpose.

Secret Five

With your imagination, you can quickly redesign and rebuild your spirit world. Your spirit world exerts irresistible, magnetic force on your physical world.

Secret Six

When your predominant feelings consist of exciting, uplifting, happy, abundant, successful and grateful feelings, you are a success... right now! As morning follows night, physical success follows spiritual success.

Secret Seven

Faith is a force for creation and is comparable to seeds. The images and scenarios you entertain in your mind grow like seeds into corresponding physical things. By using the C.A.R.T. formula you can master the art of receiving the gifts you desire.

The secrets I learned by reading the manuscript of Sultan Musa of Mali's interpretation of the metaphor of his life, Aladdin and the Magic Lamp, have been an incredible and invaluable blessing in my life. I've truly lived a magical life because of this knowledge.

It's true that I feel a deep obligation to share this information with others, because of what it did for me, but the real reason I do it is because it is incredibly fun for me! One of the greatest joys in life is watching a client's face when the reality of the Sultan's Seven Secrets sinks deep enough into their heart and mind that they **get it!** Their eyes pop open, their mouth pops open and they usually say something like, "Oh my Gosh! I see it now!"

I'm honored that you would take the time to read this book and if I can coach you to greater heights, I would be honored to do that too. I hope to see you at an Imagination Therapy Workshop or hear your voice on one of my webinars. I also encourage you to get a copy of the audio version of this book. Listening to the Sultan's Seven Secrets while driving and glancing periodically (and very quickly) at the Dream Sheets in your Dream Book can be one of life's transformative experiences.

I look forward to what you'll do as the Sultan of Your Own Destiny!

To continue your journey living the Sultan's Seven Secrets, visit **www.spellbreakerworkshop.com**

Jeff Buchner

Notes

Notes

Notes

Notes

Made in the USA
Middletown, DE
13 October 2021